Order this book at Hikermac@sbcglobal.net

Or Amazon

Copyright 2014

The views expressed in this book are solely those of the author and do not reflect the views of the publisher.

Brief portions of this book may be quoted. Otherwise permission of the author for reproduction is required.

Printed in the United States of America

ISBN-13: 978-1499160505 (CreateSpace-Assigned)
ISBN-10: 149916050X
BISAC: Biography & Autobiography / Personal Memoirs

Dedication

With Keo's permission, this book, "Remembering a Water Buffalo" is dedicated to Keo's brother,

Ko Xayavongvane.

Ko died March 17, 2014 after a short bout with pancreatic cancer.

Ko, Summer of 2013

Remembering
a Water Buffalo

Keo's Story

Preface

This is Keo's story. But it would be inadvisable to try to write his story without acknowledging and recognizing that as I write the story I cannot possibly be objective. I am intimately and passionately involved.

An important perspective as you read: Keo has consented to share some very personal information. He has, in the past, kept some aspects of his life very quiet. This story – his story – is a 'coming out' in-depth.

Keo and I met in the fall of 1986. He was hospitalized – and as a case manager for a local health clinic, I was assigned to visit him. He had been diagnosed with HIV/AIDS. It was at a time in the epidemic when the hospital nurse aids, food staff, and cleaning crew might be inclined to leave his lunch outside the door, or completely cover themselves with protective paraphernalia, or try to avoid answering the call bell. So I was a visitor that he could count on to try to help him to deal with medical language problems, the new information about the disease, the very threatening and unfamiliar hospital environment, and the agency that would, over the next 25 years, keep him connected to his doctors, health care, and state and federal pro-grams.

Keo's English language skills at that time were minimal. In addition, many of his Lao friends were apprehensive about visiting in a hospital. So he had few visitors. He was cautious, at first, about accepting me. From the time of that first visit, and for the weeks following, I was his case manager.

Eventually he became a friend of the family – and then, ten years later, after my wife and I had separated, Keo and I started dating.

The experience of dating - and loving - a Laotian man was quite an unusual experience. I had only begun to identify myself publicly as a gay man.

We certainly had our cultural and life differences. I was 22 years older.

I had post-graduate work – and he had hardly finished the equivalent of high school. I came from a marriage of 38 years. He had never married.

I had not been an active homosexual. He had always known himself as gay.

I was a career professional. In Laos he had been a student and a farmer. In the Elgin area, he held factory assembly jobs and had hotel cleaning and laundry responsibilities.

The United States was my birth country. He had entered the States as a refugee, didn't even hold a green card at first, and was not yet a US citizen.

I was a practicing Christian – and had been a minister with denominational local and national positions. He was a practicing Buddhist.

I had traveled extensively inside and outside of the United States. His primary travel experience was from the refugee camp to the United States.

Would the difference in our backgrounds and our lives make a partnership unfeasible and impossible? When we first lived together in 1999 in our own home there was, undoubtedly, some caution for each of us about believing or expecting or hoping that the relationship would last.

As I sit this day and write, we have been living in that same house – together – for fifteen years. If life and living go on as I hope they will, this summer we will celebrate with friends and family our fifteen years in this home.

Ralph McFadden

Introduction

Because of and following the Vietnam War which raged from 1959 through April 30, 1975, thousands of refugees fled Vietnam, Cambodia and Laos.

During the 1960s the U.S. fought a secret war in parts of Laos to sever the North Vietnamese supply line known as the Ho Chi Minh Trail. By 1970, two thirds of the eastern border and northeast corner of Laos had been massively bombed, causing widespread environmental destruction and the flight of 600,000 refugees, 20 percent of the total population of Laos.

Because of the war and the infiltration of Communism, there was an immigration of the indigenous lowland Laotians to several different countries, many of them heading to and arriving in the U.S. from 1979 to 1982. Keo was from one of the lowland provinces.

For background on this book, current estimates suggest there are nearly 6,000 Laotians living in Illinois with 517 in Chicago, 1,190 in Rockford and over 4,000 in Elgin and nearby areas like Hanover Park, Streamwood, South Elgin, St. Charles, Carpentersville and Algonquin. This figure, like many across the US, is believed to be undercounted.

The average income is believed to be about $42,000, with many from the first generation working in factories, while second-generation Laotians who have more education and better English skills and experience are working in more skilled office and store professions.

Currently, there are six major Wat Lao (Buddhist temples) in Illinois: 3 in Elgin, 1 in Hampshire and 2 in Rockford.

There are several known Lao organizations in Illinois including Lao American Organization of Illinois, the Lao American Community Center, Lao American Community Services, Lao Community Health Project and the Southeast Asian Youth Program at the YWCA of Elgin.

Remembering a Water Buffalo

A Story - 1998

A wonderful and humorous story captures some of the contrasts of Keo's life. Following a vacation trip to Denver to see me, Keo returned home to Elgin and was picked up at the airport by Dan, my nephew. Getting back home brought back the reality of day-by-day living. As he arrived back at his apartment parking lot, he checked on his cherished sport car. Oh, no! A flat! What a welcome home!

Two days later, because of a change in signs at an intersection near his apartment, he made an illegal left turn. His reward for that mistake was a $100 fine. That's two.

And again, two days after that, driving back from the grocery store, his car was hit – right rear – by a vehicle trying to 'hurry' an intersection. That's three.

That evening, unhappy and sad, he called me in Denver. He related the events of the week. He sighed. His frustration was evident. Perhaps with a longing for the simpler life and wondering how it was back home in Laos, he reflected, "*Sometimes I wish I was riding a water buffalo.*"

The Early Years

Kongkeo Xayavongvane was born in 1955 in Ban Sehak, a small village just south of Savannakhet, the second largest city in Laos. During his childhood and into his teenage years, he was lovingly surrounded by his family: his father and mother, three brothers, and three sisters. Together the children played with relatives and friends not only from their own village but also from near-by villages. And they worked, even as children, as soon as they were able, on the family farm – a property of several hectares (acres) of rice paddies.

Keo's village 2008

Beginning in 1999, Keo and I traveled to Laos four times over a period of nine years. On one of our trips when we visited the village of his birth, he reminded me, as we saw children playing on the dusty yard, that now I could see him as a boy, for, he noted, in some ways very little had changed. The little girls of the village helped by carrying water on their shoulder yokes, helped to cook and keep the cooking fires burning, and sometimes played with their toys. The little boys brought in firewood, dug for insects in the ground for dinner that evening, and moved the water buffaloes to different places for grazing.

They occasionally were allowed to go fishing. They also helped with the laundry by washing the clothes by hand in a large basins. The water was carried from a barrel of

11

water beside the house. The barrel was kept full by the children bringing the water from a nearby pond.

During the dry season the children – boys and girls – walked on the dusty, dry streets to school, and either come home for lunch or carried a woven basket holding sticky rice and perhaps a couple of green vegetables.

On those same streets they played games: tossing their sandals toward a target circle, or playing a form of kick-ball, or learning the skill of sending a small wicker ball over a net . . . using only their feet. I could see Keo there 45 years ago … dirty feet, dirty face, dirty shorts … and, as Keo, said, "Contented." He knew no other life. During the wet season when the children were needed to help to plow and cultivate the fields, and plant the rice, the school (below) had its vacation time.

As a part of the farming, the family owned water buffaloes. Keo's job, often, was to lead one of the water buffalo as it pulled a plow or cultivator through the water and mud of the rice paddy. And sometimes it was

possible, both for pleasure and for work, to ride on the back of the animal, clutching its massive back with his bare knees and hanging on to the strong broad neck.

Because the water buffalo was slow, deliberate, and gentle, it was not dangerous. It was, in fact, pleasant and fun.

In the early 60's when Keo was a child, there were 28 homes in Ban Sehak, less than 200 people. All were rice farmers. There were likely family secrets, but there was very little public sharing. Folks were quiet and reserved . . . that was the cultural norm. There was not much sharing of personal information.

His family lived on the second floor of a house built on stilts.

Keo's sister's house in 1999

The open underside of the house was for the farm animals, such as chickens, ducks, and pigs. The water buffaloes were usually out in the open grazing in a grassy area or in a rice paddy when the harvest was over. When Keo was young there were not many thieves - and the river was a barrier that kept the buffalo from meandering. Neighbors looked out for each other when it came to caring for the animals.

The picture below is Keo's sister's house – under development in 2008.

The picture below shows a covered kitchen, a bathroom, and laundry room being added.

The home, when Keo was a boy, had an outdoor kitchen attached to the house positioned under a corrugated metal roof. One of the three open sides was closed off with a bamboo curtain to protect the fire and the cook from the wind and the rain. The cooking was done (and it is often true today) on an open charcoal fire. Every morning the air in the village was dense with the fragrant smoke from the early breakfast cooking.

Now, in 2014, there is also a well (below), a dish for receiving TV, a rice hauler for processing new rice, and a finished lower floor living space.

The roof of Keo's home when he was a boy was often several layers of pampas grass, the walls were some kind of leaves or bamboo, and the floor for the poor was also bamboo. Some had lumber for the walls and floor. Keo recalled that their home had lumber. And in his family's situation, they had a corrugated roof.

On the 2nd floor there were small rooms for Keo and the brothers, sisters, and parents - separated by bamboo walls. The light inside the home at night was a torch light, using oil from a palm tree, mixing the oil with leaves and making a torch about a foot long called a Kabong. Or sometimes there was simply a wick in a bottle.

The diet for the family consisted of everything that was not poisonous. They raised vegetables: lettuce, corn, cucumbers, long beans, squash, sweet potatoes, onion, garlic, wild mushrooms, hot peppers and herbs for seasonings. There were also fruits: bananas, papaya, mangoes, jack fruit, oranges, lemons, pomegranates, and grapefruit. There were a great variety of insects, fish, frogs, and crabs . . . and always the daily staple of sticky rice.

Despite that rather long list . . . the family sometimes did not have enough to eat. If the wet and growing season was not successful and plentiful, a family could run out of rice. Fruits and vegetables were available if the growing season was good, and if the family had the money needed to buy in the market. Sometimes it was possible, depending on the success of the growing season to sell rice, or, if needed, it might be necessary to borrow or buy rice from another family member or a neighbor.

When he was born, Keo had four older siblings. Later, two younger siblings – a brother and a sister – were added to the family. One child, a brother, died at birth when Keo was 13 years old.

Pictured is Keo (second from right) with sisters and Brothers in 1999.

Keo was very sick and frail when he was 8 or 9. So sick that his mother, who often was also sick, found it diffi-cult to care for him. His brothers and sisters helped with his care. He was small and fragile because of his illness. Keo's mother died in 1966 when Keo was 11. With his mother's death Keo and his family took on even more and greater responsibilities. Keo regained health and strength in his teenage years.

Dongsavanh, Keo, Ko and Kam in 2008

The family, like at least 80% of the country, were Buddhists. There was a temple (or called a wat) in a neighboring village. That temple area was also the home to a few monks.

When Keo's mother died, and many years later when his father died, the family and the village gathered with the monks to hold a service of commemoration in very traditional Buddhist services. It was a common practice for monks and friends from surrounding village to come to the services. (Picture is a service in 2008).

For several days Keo's mother's body was laid out in a wooden casket and kept in the home. Then the casket

was carried to the cemetery and the body cremated.

Picture is Keo's father's cremation.

Visiting his father's and sister's shrines in 1988

In accordance with the cultural and religious tradition, 100 days after the death of the loved one, there would be a blessing and ceremony with food, chants and then dancing. The costs were borne by the family and with monetary and food gifts from others. Often the wealthier families would have an elaborate celebration, and sometimes more than one.

After his mother's body had been cremated, the ashes were present for the ceremony – and a few days later the family and friends took the ashes to the grave, a shrine or stupa -- an ornate temple-like structure. His mother's shrine was situated between the family rice paddies and the river.

When Keo visited that site 35 years later, he discovered that the floods from the river had washed away the embankment and the shrine was no longer there.

The schools, which Keo attended from first grade to the sixth, were in two separate sites close to his village and neighboring villages. There were about 60 children in the first three grades in one building. That school was a short distance from Keo's village. From fourth to sixth he was in another school in another village – and there were about 100 children who attended. The teachers in the schools were from surrounding villages. All teachers were educated and had gone to training school.

In school the subjects were math, reading and writing, painting and drawing; and from fourth grade up there were classes in French. The children learned at an early age that Laos had been a colony of France. Laotians also learned Thai as they often listened on battery operated radios.

In the village when Keo was a boy there was no electricity. There were no wells. The bathroom was the rice paddy or a close-by wooded area. Baths were taken by pouring water over oneself from a nearby pond. The bather was adept at keeping a towel around himself or herself while bathing. It was understood that you did not try to invade the privacy by looking – hoping to get a sneak look at a naked person. One did not pay attention because the culture conditioned the child and adult to be blind to such personal hygiene. Keo is, to this day, reserved when it comes to bathing.

Water for cooking and for drinking came from that same bathing pond. That pond, not incidentally, was also the watering post for some of the animals of the area.

Several times a day the children would carry the water from the pond to their homes – about the length of two football fields - in pails hung on yokes on their shoulders. The picture – below - in 2008 indicates that little has changed. . the yokes are still in use. Most recently some of the village homes now have wells and electric pumps. Perhaps, in time, the child carrying water in pails on shoulders will be a chore of the past.

History Lesson

Part of the ongoing history of Laos – for centuries – has been the invasions of the country by bordering neighbors and colonializing European nations.

The Vietnam/US war was no exception. Keo and his family and the many Lao villages, unwillingly and with later severe consequences for Keo and his brother Ko, were the 'beneficiaries' of the Viet Nam war.

Keo recalls when he was ten or eleven seeing US bombers from the Savannakhet airport and from Thailand flying overhead east toward Viet Nam.

US bombers over Viet Nam - Ho Chin Min Trail - 1966

Often they flew northeast to the province of Houaphon Province where the Ho Chi Minh trail came from the north in China, through the northeast corner of Laos, south toward South Vietnam. There, in that province, they dropped bombs on the landscape of the Xieng Khouang plateau - the trails, the fields, the farms, the villages, the ancient Plain of Jars - to try stop the Vietnamese and Communist soldiers from going south.

Keo's village people saw the planes fly overhead, and about 20 to 30 minutes later heard the bombs exploding, and then saw the empty planes returning.

(See Appendix for more information on the war and the bombings.)

**2013 - Today the bombed fields still remain.
Unexploded bombs are a daily hazard for children.**

In his mid-teens, during the continuation of the US/Vietnam war, Keo went into Savannakhet to live with his brother and attend the upper grades. It was a little unusual for a younger child to leave the village and move into the city. Keo's family was sort of in the middle between being very poor and being a little better off. Venturing into the city to live with his brother was indeed adventurous. It was all very new to him.

Keo's older brother, the one who lived in Savannakhet, was a soldier. All of his adult life he was in the regular military. As a soldier he kept a low profile, trying to keep out of the increasingly difficult politics of the city and of the country.

In the city Keo rode his bike to school and attended the upper grades. He had friends his own age and when not in school they roamed over the growing city. For leisure and for a little spending money he, along with his friends, sold lottery tickets along the roadside. Once in a while he and his family and friends would enjoy a festival at the local wat or temple.

When Keo lived in the city, his sister, Kam, was in the family village. She was going through her own health problems. She had children at home and, at that time, very little income. Part of Keo's earnings from selling lottery tickets would go to his sister.

While living in Savannakhet Keo had an enjoyable experience of auditioning for a local radio singing contest. Unfortunately, as it happened, the tower of the radio station was destroyed in a storm and the radio station contest ended. Perhaps his whole life would have been different if he would have won. Nowadays Keo can be heard, in the house or in the garden, singing softly some of his favorite tunes.

And the war continued.

For the people of Laos there were always wars. For centuries Laos was often in conflict with its neighbors who wished to add Laotian territory to their own national lands. Keo's misfortune was to be raised at a time when there were conflicts all over Southeast China -- in Viet Nam, Cambodia, and Laos. And when the United States left Southeast Asia in 1975, following the lost war with Viet Nam, most of the government, today called The People's Republic of Laos, supported the invasion by Communists and encouraged Communism in the nation. They were promised, by the Communists, a good bit of independence for their culture and their own style of governing. They found out, in time, that the reassurance of that independence was not forth-coming.

The tension in the country grew as the China-backed Communists took over the politics of Laos. There was disagreement for the citizens of the country about the involvement of the Communists not only in the government, but also as it touched the lives of the villagers. The Communists taught their doctrine – and wanted the people of Laos to understand and accept that philosophy and way of life. And if a person, parti-cularly a leader, did not like what was happening, then that person was ostracized or was sent someplace for indoctrination (brainwashing) . . . to understand the true meaning and promises of life under Communism.

It was a collective story that the King of Laos and his family did not meet the criteria imposed by communist government. They – the whole family – were sent to seminars – and were not heard from again.

Keo, and his younger brother, Ko, did not like the Communist intrusion into the village and into their lives. At first they played along, that is, they were quiet, in order to survive. Then they learned about the movement of guerillas from some older soldiers from the city who came out to the village because they did not want to attend the Communist seminars. These soldiers were being forced, in the city, to go to the training and brain-washing seminars. From those disgusted and defiant soldiers, Keo and Ko learned to know about the guerillas that had fled the city and had taken up residence in the surrounding woods and jungles.

In 1975 Keo and Ko, as anti-communists, along with many other young adult men, also fled into the jungles and joined the forces of independent guerillas. They lived on sticky rice, fish, vegetables, bamboo shoots, water snail, insects, and any wild animals they could find such as birds and lizards. Villagers would sometimes bring them food. There were no big wild animals in the jungles – the isolated areas - because they had been hunted and killed over the years and they were gone.

For the most part they were unsuccessful guerillas and soon realized that they must flee their home and country. Keo and Ko, during the rainy season and despite the flooded Mekong River, with the aid of

banana tree logs, escaped one night from Laos by swimming across the Mekong River into Thailand.

They were willingly received by the Thai people and escorted by the Thai government into the Ubon Ratchathani refugee camp, one of two large refugee camps in Thailand. Keo and Ko lived there for three years along with hundreds of others.

The time in the refugee camp was crucial for Keo. It certainly was an adventure. It was a time for exploring a part of his life that had been kept very quiet in the village. Keo met some young men his age who would become life-long friends. It was a time for being open about being gay. Several friends − in that setting − cross-dressed. That is, they dressed as young women. It became a way of identifying themselves as unique and feminine. In that refugee setting, Keo joined in on that new way of living.

In later years, in the United States, a number of those friends took the medical steps needed to become transgendered. Keo did not wish to make such a decision.

Years later, after Keo had moved to the United States, he learned that many of his friends had similar refugee camp stories. Pine, Kim, Seng, Samay, Manivanh . . . all went through refugee camps and came to the US in in the late 70's and early 80's. They all had the difficult experience of having to escape from Laos. One couldn't simply walk away. They had to escape at night. They might escape with a group. Sometimes they came as a family. For instance, Samay's whole family came. Samay came as a young man. She was about 18 or 19. Later, Samay was one of Keo's friends who became trans-gendered. She is still a good friend.

Friends would talk with each other and dream of another country and another opportunity. Keo said that it was scary, and yet he was excited about starting a new life.

< Thai Refugee camp image

In their third year at the refugee camp, Keo and Ko were given the oppor-tunity to select the country where they would like to live. They chose the United States and were transferred to a refugee camp in the Philippines where they stayed for three months.

Moving to Elgin, Illinois

The last leg of this major journey was from the Philippines to Church World Service in Houston, Texas, for placement in the United States. Then, because a friend had moved to Elgin and the YWCA of Elgin was willing to sponsor them, Keo and Ko landed in northern Illinois.

The movement to Elgin from Houston must have been both exciting and frightening. The friend from Elgin had sent the brothers a little cash. They did not then understand the value of American money: a quarter, a dollar, or five dollars. The friend also sent Keo and Ko one-way bus tickets to Elgin. They would, on this bus adventure, arrive in Elgin via Union Station in Chicago.

They arrived at the Chicago Union Station near midnight and were ushered off the bus, were given their luggage, and were on their own. Keo had a phone number of the friend in Elgin. He had a quarter, which he understood he could use for the call. He dialed the Elgin number – and got - not his Lao friend - but a woman's voice saying something he could not understand. He tried several times – with no success. The operator was, apparently, asking him to put in more money. It was not a local call, but a long distance call.

No ticket booths in the station were open. There was no one from Church World Service or the YWCA to meet them. Fortunately, while despairing on what to do, Keo showed his ticket to a night-time custodian. The custodian led them to a gate – pointed to the ticket and the gate – and with his fingers indicated that the bus would be there at 7 a.m. It worked. Hours later Ko and Keo pulled into the Elgin depot, were told that this was the place to get off, pulled out the quarter – and this time they reached their friends.

And so the new life began

Despite the major shift from village to city, from playing children's games in the dust in the village to TV's, sports cars, and fast food, Keo adapted to this new culture, as did his brother and many Lao friends. Elgin, Illinois became home for thousands of Laotians. Within the first ten years, through classes, tests, inter-views and patience, Keo became a citizen of the United States.

Keo and Ralph Celebrate Citizenship

During the early years in Elgin and the greater Chicago area, Keo attended English classes, developed job-hunting skills, learned to survive the winters, received a green card through the auspices of the YWCA, got a

35

driver's license, paid taxes, earned enough income to buy a car, commuted with others or by himself to a factory or to a hotel job, and most often lived with one to three others in order to share the rent of an apartment.

Keo as a young man in Elgin

One remarkable and unforgettable part of the story is that Keo and some of the same friends he had learned to know in the Thai camp, traveled into Chicago for fun and gay experiences. And often Keo carried out that part of his life in drag. And so did many of his friends. Why in drag? For some it felt more feminine. For Keo, as he learned, the white male married or unmarried men wanted the gay sex but were more attracted to a brown skinned slightly built female figure – even knowing that that attractive female was, in fact, a young man.

Yes, it is Keo

So goes the fantasy. Of interest – unlike the Christian communities - the Buddhist communities had no spoken or written condemnation of the cross dressing or the male same-sex attraction. Such criticism was not a part of Keo's life experience at that time. Many changes took place in those early years in Elgin. Several of the young men decided to undergo sex changes. That is, through surgery they moved from male to female genitalia. Such surgery was available in Chicago, in San Francisco and, for less cost, in Bangkok.

It was undoubtedly during some of those Chicago area gay escapades that Keo was infected with HIV. And so were many of his friends.

37

In the eighties HIV/AIDS was not known about by most of the gay community. It was silently developing as a pandemic globally and an epidemic nationally, and even when it began to be known that there was a disease, it was not understood.

 And because it was taking place and happening in the gay community, it was a shadow disease – and, after all, "they deserved it." The religious communities could only cast cruel disparaging remarks. The good folks in the political arena refused to acknowledge its existence. **Pictured below: Keo on lower right with three friends. Only Keo survived the HIV.**

Keo, through the excellent support of the Open Door Clinic, a Fox Valley STD agency, found medical support from several caring physicians. He was under the watchful care of his first case manager. That case manager became, years later, his life partner.

Keo at AIDS Quilt in DC

Keo was soon taking the primary drug available at the time – AZT. It sometimes worked, but for most men and women diagnosed with AIDS the drug was a deterrent only for a short time before the patient succumbed with one of the many debilitating and fatal diseases: respiratory, sarcoma, brain tumor, cancer, weight loss, and so forth. Keo had been diagnosed with PCP – pneumocystis pneumonia – the disease that affected about 75% of those with HIV. He was one of the fortunate ones who survived because of the meds, the support he received, and his own amazingly positive attitude.

During those years in the late eighties and throughout the nineties many of Keo's friends died: Mone moved back to Laos to be with his family in his final days; Connie (transgendered) left her family in Elgin and fled to San Francisco and drugs; and Tui traveled to San Diego – where he died in a few years. Keo can recall at least ten of his Lao gay friends who did not make it through the AIDS epidemic.

 Keo kept the information about his life-threatening disease to himself. Though local friends may have suspected, it was not something that he or many of his infected friends shared with friends or family. In the 90's such information was strictly confidential. And being silent about the disease was not only a matter of confidentiality but also it was very congruent with the Lao culture. It was a personal medical matter. It was not the kind of information shared with friends or family. Keo was alone on this journey – but, fortunately, he had the support of Open Door.

Keo's life in Elgin was fairly routine: finding work, buying a car, sharing an apartment with friends, cooking Lao food together with groceries from one of several Lao stores, shopping at a mall, getting a credit card or two, having Lao community gatherings and celebrations, and attending, on occasion, a Buddhist temple service.

The Lao community from the greater Elgin area, with the support of the monks, had home blessings, celebrated weddings, births and funerals.

The gathered community spent time listening to Laotian music, singing along with Thai and Lao karaoke, reminiscing about the times back home, greeting friends who might come from another part of the United States to visit, and finding ways to communicate with the friends and family back in Laos.

They were remembering the water buffalo.

Communicating with home was not easy. On one occasion, in the mid-80's, Keo's father asked to talk with him. So it was arranged. His father had to travel eight hours to Bangkok, and there by pre-arrangement, wait for a few days for Keo to get the correct information, and then make a phone call to the home of a Lao family living in Bangkok.

Most transplanted Laotians in the states wished to send money to their families back home. That financial communication was also difficult. In the early years Keo had an arrangement to send certified checks to banks in Savannakhet, and then his brother, who lived there, could pick up the money if he had appropriate identification.

Families, back in Laos, were often dependent on the financial support of the ones in the States. For the most part, the family members in the United States, now more affluent than they had ever been, willingly sent money back home. In fact, many of the folks who came to the US did so with the anticipation and expectation that they could make money to send home. It was not unusual for the husband/father to come to this country for a few years – in order to provide support for those in Laos.

Travel

Keo's life in the 90's did include some traveling to many states by car and by plane. One of his 'white' friends lived in Oregon. That same friend took him on a trip to Florida.

But his life changed rapidly when he came to Colorado and we started developing a serious relationship. We became travelers visiting Rocky Mountain National Park, Yellowstone National Park, the Tetons, and the Grand Canyon.

Over the 18 years of our relationship we vacationed and traveled through 45 of the 48 continental states. Rocky Mountain National Park, Yellowstone, and the Tetons were visited more than once. Regular visits were made to California, Arizona, Colorado, New Mexico, and Florida. Getting away from the winter in Illinois became an annual event.

Oregon beach

Mt. Evans... 14,200 ft.

Traveling to Laos

Chief among our travels were four trips to Laos. Usually the trip was two or three weeks over there. The last trip in 2008 was four weeks long.

Those trips took on an expected sameness. Most of the time was spent visiting family. The first trip included Keo's two older sisters and the youngest brother. A later visit also included an older brother.

Keo's visit was always anticipated by his family with high expectations. Keo was expected to see and visit with as many family members as possible. There were dinners, tours of the farms, checking out the businesses just started by his brother, touring Savannakhet and the surrounding provinces by tuk-tuk, visiting temples, seeing parks even his family had not seen, checking out new homes and urban developments , and national historic sites. The two pictures following are the renouned ancient ruin - Wat Phou in Champasak Province; and the That Luang temple in Vientianne.

Keo's Lao Family

Even with the life in the US, and living with a partner, Keo's life has remained focused on his Laotian family and home. He *does remember the water buffalo*.

An indication of that long-distant but very important connection has been his financial support for his family over the many years he has lived in the States.

His monthly financial gifts have included support for English lessons for his nieces, a truck driver's school and credentials for a nephew, advanced training for a niece in banking, and support for medical care for a number of members of the family.

Rice Huller – used by the whole village

On a more significant financial level, there has been the purchase of two smaller farms for rice production, a tractor for those fields, a rice huller, a satellite dish for

the TV, and the digging of a well for his sister.

He paid for the construction of a home for his brother (**picture above**), and a remodeling and updating of his sister's home. Help was also given for a three-wheeled taxi, bikes for the children, and monthly general support for daily living.

The Taxi

Remembering the Water Buffalo

Refugees – singling and in families – came to the United States hoping to start a new life.

There were restrictions, but once here it was possible to have parents or a wife or children come and join the newly transplanted refugee.

It was not easy. Statistics – over a period of forty years – have shown that males, who used to be employed in Laos in vocations for which they were trained, now found it difficult to find suitable work. And some of those who failed to find satisfying work chose the route of alcoholism, serious health issues, and suicide. Some returned home.

Parents, brought over by resolute and determined adult children, found it impossible to learn the language or the culture. They could not drive, did not shop or even know where to shop, did not understand the language, and were afraid of banks, law enforcement and medical agencies. There was no such thing as a daily trip to the open market to buy fresh farm produce, or buy a freshly slaughtered chicken. They found themselves isolated in their children's homes watching a TV – with language and images totally unfamiliar.

Is it any wonder that they *"remembered the water buffalo?"* How do I get back to that which is my home?

Mone – with AIDS – went home to die. *He remembered the water buffalo.*

 An older woman down the street from us, left her children in the US and returned home to a very small village with its close-by open market with produce spread on a tarp, with the familiar language on the radio or even on a TV. She is back home and all is now safe and familiar. *She remembered, fondly, the water buffalo.*

Pine, having lived here in the United States since 1980, has had a good job with pension benefits, and will soon to be retirement age with Social Security benefits. She wishes to sell her home and go back to Laos to live with family – even without Medicare support. *She remembers the water buffalo.*

Here in Elgin, on a very regular basis, a few hundred Lao folks will participate in a local wat/temple celebration, with chanting of the monks, and selling fruits and vegetables that were familiar in the markets of Lao. And such a celebration is, of course, in part, *remembering the water buffalo.*

Mentioned earlier there were and are the many times that the community gets together for Lao dinners and food. All of the familiar: egg rolls, spring rolls, hot papaya salads, sticky rice, pork fried rice, tangy sweet and sour soups, and coconut flavored desserts. A pleasant time – often *remembering the water buffalo.*

In the early years of being in the US the Lao community would come together frequently. As time passed, the families dispersed, many moved because of other friends, or marriage, or work, or wishing for a changed climate. Some became "better off" financially – and pulled away from the familiar community. They were searching for a new and wider community. Some wished for more identity with their new upscale white culture. Some wished to break away from an identity with their old life. *They, perhaps, did not want to remember the water buffalo.*

Dongsavanh, Keo and Ko - near the village 2008

Keo and Dongsavahn visiting shrine of older brother.

Visiting the family rice fields

The Most Recent years

Keo has a life now – with both cultures. He maintains contact locally with many Lao friends: buying at one of the local Lao grocery stores, seeing at least one of his friends almost daily – speaking Lao, seeing Thai news stations or Lao videos, cooking his favorite Lao foods.

Keo communicates every other week with his sister and brother in Laos. It is amazing how the phone communication has changed. In 1999, when Keo would try to call his brother in Savannakhet, he would need to call a neighbor who had a landline. Then the neighbor would be given 30 minutes to go next door to find Keo's brother, Dongsavanh. Then Keo would call again. Calls were $2.50 a minute – the best ATT overseas rate to Laos at that time.

Now one can buy a phone card from a gas station or Lao grocery store, and make a sixty minute call for $2.00. And Keo can even call his sister Kam in her village which has no phone service. She uses her cell phone.

In Keo's Two Worlds

Keo not only keeps in touch with his Lao roots, but also has a foot firmly in his American country.

He has an old, loved and very well cared-for BMW.

That car, of course, has insurance to pay, Illinois license tags, servicing by a reliable auto company, and always gas. . . that can never be as inexpensive as it was when he bought his first car.

And he has a white American life partner. We have been in a relationship for over fifteen years. He cooks his Lao food, but also grills chicken, hamburgers and steaks. The two of us eat out regularly at inexpensive fast food sites, or small very American restaurants.

Keo watches TV. That has been a great asset for he continually learns his English from "Wheel of Fortune," "Jeopardy," talk shows, ABC News, and evening drama and action shows. Our TV has access to YouTube through a hookup with our computer – so he can frequently see very recent videos from Laos on HDTV.

He has learned to use both the desk top and laptop computer focusing on emails, Facebook, and YouTube. He is frequently in touch with Lao friends all over the United States. And on weekends, especially on Sunday morning, he can be, via the chat room on Facebook, in touch with his niece or nephew in Savannakhet. He has become well known by many Lao and 'white' friends for his regular postings and garden pictures on Facebook.

He has the burdens of any American household: taxes to pay, keeping up with his social security, and being connected to health care. For the most part, his life is good – and contented.

The Garden Sanctuary

Of great significance to Keo is our garden. When we first moved in 1999 to our present home, the backyard was very bland. Almost all undernourished grass. There were two trees: a dying Ash and a huge, lovely bur oak. And a rusty swing set.

We started developing the yard and garden. Each year there were new additions to the yard: a brick patio, a small two tier pond – sometimes with fish, then a twenty five foot long raised area for flowers, many shrubs, small fruit trees, a vegetable garden, a shed, a cover for the patio, a stream to a larger Koi pond, a

Buddha garden, and always – more and more flower beds.

Keo's outdoor love from March through October is the lawn and the garden. There is an early morning time when he leisurely walks through the garden. It is a time of meditation, observing the changes, the new buds, considering next plantings, where to place the pots, the statues, the hanging baskets. It is his quiet time.

Throughout the day there will be weeding, cutting back dead materials, watching the birds and their nests, noting where an animal has dug in the lawn, or where some animals have established a path through our yard going to another yard.

Keo, during some of my illnesses, has taken over the care of the lawn – the mowing and the trimming. I am allowed to do the upkeep of the lawn by fertilizing.

You can see some of the still pictures above, – and if you wish you can look *up* the three 4 minute videos of the garden for the last three summers. You can see, on YouTube, the three videos:

2011 garden: go to   ***Keosgarden yt***

2012 garden: go to   ***Our Summer Garden 2012***

2013 garden: go to   ***Keo's Garden 2013***

September 2013

A major part of Keo's life here in the states has been his relationship to Ko, his younger brother. The connection has been of great significance.

Dongsavanh, Ko and Keo - 2008

They grew up together as boys. Attended school together, worked on the farm, enjoyed their family life, and then took the long journey of leaving Laos and coming to the United States. Through it all Ko was a constant and reliable friend and brother. Keo and Ko shared about work and daily living. Together they shared ideas and made plans about connecting with their family in Laos. I recall with some clarity sitting in Ko's living room. Keo and I talked with Ko about our first planned trip back to Laos, Savannakhet and the village. What to take, what to expect, and who to see.

Ko and Keo: years of growing up together, fleeing Laos, and being immersed into a new and completely foreign environment. And they made it. It all worked out.

Then came a disturbing phone call to Keo one morning in early September. It was a terrible shock. Out of nowhere, with no early prognosis, Ko called Keo after a visit to his doctor. He had not been feeling well. In a scan of the abdomen, a small 3 cm mass was found on the pancreas. The immediate diagnosis was pancreatic cancer.

We knew, because of a similar recent history of a friend, that this prognosis was not good. Few persons survived pancreatic cancer for more than a year. Even with the wondrous progress of medical science, there were very few treatment options, and none were guaranteed to work out.

Keo talked with his brother – and with friends. The news did not sink in immediately. Keo admitted that he did not understand, he was frozen by the thought, and he did not believe that there were so few options for treatment.

Through the hope and the persuasion of daughter Linda, Ko, in a courageous and hope-filled move, agreed to go to the Cancer Treatment Centers of America hospital in Zion, Illinois. The Treatment Center paid the airfare from Minneapolis to Milwaukee, and the limo service to Zion. Linda had Googled for treatment options, found promise in NanoKnive, a minimally invasive treatment for cancer. The Center, when asked about it, encouraged the family by holding out hope. The week in Zion was, in many ways, a nightmare. Ko, struggling with breathing problems and some of the early pain of the cancer, though staying in a nearby hotel, was in and out of emergency care in the hospital. Finally, after 8 days of interviewing, x-raying, probing and coming up with no connection whatsoever to NanoKnife, Ko and Xeuam went back home.

The at-home visits to the oncologist, to the clinic, and to first one hospital and then to another began and continued. The prognosis was not good. But Ko and the family were fighters.

Ko and Keo were on the phone almost every day . . . often twice a day. Even when Ko was fatigued. Even when Ko could hardly talk.

Keo and I had visited Ko in Zion – then weeks later began to make the seven hour, 400 mile one-way trip to

Minneapolis. . not once, but several times. Those visits came closer together as the weeks passed – and then in the final three weeks of Ko's life, we made the trip weekly.

Without detailing the final details of the days of suffering, several scenarios stand out:

Seeing Ko in an intensive care unit with oxygen mask, losing weight, often able to eat only a teaspoon of soup – and vomiting within a few seconds.

Seeing Ko's wife suffering the emotional pain as she stayed by his bedside most nights, resting sometimes on a bedside reclining chair, sometimes balled up in a blanket in a visitor's room, always willing to be there.

Keo standing by the bed, talking in Laotian to his oxygen-masked brother. Sometimes leaving the room in order to hide his tears.

Frequently supporting Xeuam when she is in tears . . . taken a break and has moved out to the hallway.

And then, in the final three days, we traveled one last time to Abbott Northwestern Hospital, parked in the adjacent multi-storied garage, and stood by Ko's bedside in an ICU room. Xeuam was there. And daughter Linda with her husband Yoom and their 3 year old daughter Trinity. And their quiet seventeen year old son, Vinny. And Keo . . . and I.

We were there when the palliative care doctor so carefully, clearly and compassionately talked with Ko, Xeuam, and Keo, naming the options. There were only two. Take off the CPAP breathing mask – and die. Or intubate – and struggle for a couple of days hoping for a miracle. Initially Ko opted for the former. Then, after he and the family had said their goodbyes --- and Keo and I drove the 400 miles back home, Ko and the immediate family decided to try one last time – and on Saturday evening he was attached by intubation to a ventilator. Less than 48 hours later it was accepted that there was no improvement. The last of the life extending medical paraphernalia equipment was removed. At 3:00 a.m. on the 17th of March, 2014, Ko left this earth-bound journey.

That morning, at about 9:00 a.m., we drove back, not to the hospital, but to the Minneapolis suburb, Brooklyn Park. To Ko's home.

Keo had a job to do. He was asked by Xeuam to be at the home . . . help to receive visitors, collect and record their monetary gifts, and pay some of the bills.

From that Monday evening and for the next seven days, family and friends flocked to the home.

They brought their presence, contributions of food, money, and memories.

There were three monks from a close-by temple – and they were there for ceremonies for five of the seven days.

The living room furniture and dining room table had been moved to the side. The carpeted floor was covered with several more colorful sitting blankets for the monks as they carried out the chanting rituals, the lighting of candles, the lifting of the 'alms' for the blessing of the monks. The carpeted areas often were crowded not only with the family and friends, but also with silver bowls of fruit, contributions of tokens of money, baskets of sticky rice, sweets, and the rudiments of the ritual.

When the monks were not present, the family and friends could be seen sitting on the area rugs, eating or talking, and sometimes playing cards. The purpose . . . always the purpose . . . was to be there, in the home, present to the ones suffering the loss.

On Sunday morning, the final ritual services took place in a chapel at a local cemetery. Family and friends gathered for the ceremony. There was an open casket, and there were six volunteer monks and a group of volunteer nuns.

The volunteer monks in bright orange - heads shaven

Ko's son, Vinny, was one of the volunteer monks, and Ko's daughter, Linda, was one of the volunteer nuns.

Following the morning service the family, a couple of friends, and the monks took Ko's body to the crematory on the grounds of the cemetery. The family was present for the cremation.

The next morning, Monday, the family returned to the crematory – and entered into a blessing for the ashes. Then all returned to the home for the final ceremony with the monks.

In 100 days – the family and friends will come together at the home for a remembrance and blessing.

Now what?

At this writing, Keo is going on with his living. It is June and the garden is beckoning. It is time to clean up the winter debris, turn over the soil and prepare the garden for the hot Asian peppers, empty the shed of the many statues and jars and vases, clean out the upper pond, and get the fountains running. It is a time of new beginnings.

Of course, the old is not forgotten. Ko is not forgotten. Life in the village is not forgotten.

Tomorrow will come – with its uncertainties, joys, sorrows – and great expectations. Keo's life in this nation and yet, *always, he is remembering the water buffalo.*

Please stay on the path.

There are only two mistakes one can make along the road to truth; not going all the way, and not starting.
    Buddha

Do not dwell in the past, do not dream of the future, concentrate the mind on the present moment.
    Buddha

APPENDIX

Thank You

It is noted in "Remembering a Water Buffalo" that Keo is a client of the Open Door Clinic. He became a client in 1988 when he was first diagnosed with AIDS. That was twenty-seven years ago.

Keo has had the uncompromising, caring, and life-saving support of the staff at Open Door. That support has included his indomitable case manager Sharon Marach, executive David Roesler, and senior staff member Phyllis Stevens.

Some of the proceeds of the sale of this book will be contributed to the Open Door Clinic. If the reader wishes, gifts may be sent to droesler@opendoorclinic.org. Open Door notes "Our goal is to increase the quality of life of those who cannot afford to do it on their own. All donations to Open Door go toward providing the best possible care to our clients."

Keo and Ralph are thankful and deeply indebted to the on-going support of Open Door. Without it, there would be no story.

We also thank BMC – the Brethren Mennonite Council for LGBT Interests. BMC has been a friend for both Keo and Ralph. Carol Wise, the executive, has been in our home a number of times. We have always known of their support and caring.

Friends and members of The Highland Avenue Church of the Brethren, even though Keo is Buddhist, have been compassionate and caring. We are appreciative of their support in so many ways.

The US and the war – the bombings

From 1964 to 1973, the U.S. dropped more than two million tons of ordnance on seven provinces in Laos during 580,000 bombing missions—equal to a planeload of bombs every 8 minutes, 24-hours a day, for 9 years – making Laos the most heavily bombed country per capita in history. The bombings were part of the U.S. Secret War in Laos to support the Royal Lao Government against the Pathet Lao and to interdict traffic along the Ho Chi Minh Trail. The bombings destroyed many villages and displaced hundreds of thousands of Lao civilians during the nine-year period.

Up to a third of the bombs dropped did not explode, leaving Laos contaminated with vast quantities of unexploded ordnance (UXO). Over 20,000 people have been killed or injured by UXO in Laos since the bombing ceased. The wounds of war are not only felt in Laos. When the Americans withdrew from Laos in 1973, hundreds of thousands of refugees fled the country, and many of them ultimately resettled in the US.

**Regions in Laos that were bombed
are highlighted in red and yellow.**

Here are some other startling facts about the U.S. bombing of Laos and its tragic aftermath:

- Over 270 million cluster bombs were dropped on Laos during the Vietnam War (210 million more bombs than were dropped on Iraq in 1991, 1998 and 2006 combined); up to 80 million did not detonate.

- Nearly 40 years on, less than 1% of these munitions have been destroyed. More than half of all confirmed cluster munitions casualties in the world have occurred in Laos.
- Each year there continue to be over 100 new casualties in Laos. Close to 60% of the accidents result in death, and 40% of the victims are children.
- Between 1996 and 2012, the U.S. contributed on average $2.6M per year for UXO clearance in Laos; the U.S. spent $17M per day (in 2010 dollars) for nine years bombing Laos.
- The U.S. spent as much in three days bombing Laos ($51M, in 2010 dollars) than it spent for clean up over 16 years ($51M).

Laos – The World's Best Selling Guide to Laos

For a thorough study of Laos, Lonely Planet has published an excellent 375 page paperback detailing history, the government and current politics, religion, sites for the tourist, and detailed maps. Lonely Planet is available through Amazon and many book stores.

U.S. Relations with Laos

Bureau of East Asian and Pacific Affairs

August 2, 2012

U.S.-LAOS RELATIONS

The United States established diplomatic relations with Laos in 1950, following its limited independence within the French Union. Nationalists continued to push for an end to French colonialism. Laos gained full independence from France in 1954, but within a few years it entered into civil war. The United States supported a rightist regime in Laos. For nearly a decade beginning in 1964, Laos was subjected to heavy U.S. bombing as part of the wider war in Indochina. Following the change of regimes in Vietnam and Cambodia in 1975, a communist government also came to power in Laos. The government aligned itself with Vietnam and the Soviet bloc, implementing one-party rule and a command economy. U.S.-Lao relations deteriorated after 1975, and U.S. representation was downgraded. After the collapse of the Soviet Union, Laos sought to improve relations with other countries. Full U.S.-Lao diplomatic relations were restored in 1992. In July 2012 Secretary of State Hillary Clinton visited Laos, marking the first visit by a Secretary of State since 1955.

Accounting for American personnel missing in Laos from the war was the initial focus of the post-war bilateral relationship. Since that time the relationship has broadened to include cooperation on a broad range of issues including counter narcotics, health, environment, and trade.

U.S. Assistance to Laos

Following the 1986 introduction of some economic reforms, Laos' economy is essentially a free market system with active central planning by the government. The overarching policy goals for U.S. assistance to Laos are to improve Lao governance and the rule of law, and increase the country's capacity to integrate fully within

Glad you're getting a chance to
spend some time with Monica —

Love, Dan

Dad,

Here's a copy of Keo's book. Ralph said you'd just borrow someones — that you don't buy books anymore.

I figured it doesn't take up much room. And, pass it along when you're done if you choose.

I haven't read my copy yet — Ralph says there are some surprises @ Keo.

(OVER)

the Association for Southeast Asian Nations (ASEAN) and the global economy.

The largest part of U.S. bilateral assistance to Laos is devoted to improving health. The United States also helps improve trade policy in Laos, promotes sustainable development and biodiversity conservation, and works to strengthen the criminal justice system and law enforcement. Unexploded ordnance (UXO) from the war, particularly cluster munitions, remains a major problem. The United States has provided significant support for UXO clearance, removal and assistance for survivors.

Bilateral Economic Relations

U.S. exports to Laos include diamonds, metals, aircraft, vehicles, and agricultural products. U.S. imports from Laos include apparel, inorganic chemicals, agricultural products, and jewelry. Laos is working toward accession to the World Trade Organization (WTO) and has committed to joining the ASEAN Economic Community (AEC). Both of these processes require trade and regulatory reforms, which should make the investment climate more attractive to U.S. companies. WTO and AEC requirements also reinforce fuller implementation of the conditions of the 2005 U.S.-Laos bilateral trade agreement. The United States and Laos have a bilateral investment agreement and have signed a civil aviation agreement.

Laos's Membership in International Organizations

Laos and the United States belong to a number of the same international organizations, including the United Nations, ASEAN Regional Forum, International Monetary Fund, and World Bank. Laos also is an observer to the World Trade Organization.

History of the U.S. Refugee Resettlement Program

The U.S. has historically maintained a policy of admitting refugees of special humanitarian concern into the country. Following the admission of over 250,000 displaced Europeans in the wake of World War II, the first refugee legislation enacted by the U.S. Congress was the Displaced Persons Act of 1948. This legislation provided for the admission of an additional 400,000 displaced Europeans.

Later laws provided for admission of persons fleeing Communist regimes from Hungary, Poland, Yugoslavia, Korea and China, and Cuba. Most of these waves of refugees were assisted by private ethnic and religious organizations in the U.S. which formed the basis for the public/private role of U.S. refugee resettlement today.

In 1975 the U.S. resettled hundreds of thousands of Indochinese refugees through an ad hoc Refugee Task Force with temporary funding.

This experience prompted Congress to pass the Refugee Act of 1980, which incorporated the United Nations definition of "refugee" and standardized the resettlement services for all refugees admitted to the U.S.

The Refugee Act provides the legal basis for today's Refugee Admissions Program and is administered by the Bureau of Population, Refugees, and Migration (BPRM) of the Department of State in conjunction with the Office of Refugee Resettlement in the Department of Health and Human Services (HHS) and offices in the Department of Homeland Security (DHS).

The 9 U.S. Refugee Resettlement Agencies that help newly arrived refugees settle into local communities. These organizations include: Church World Service, Ethiopian Community Development Council, Episcopal Migration Ministries, Hebrew Immigrant Aid Society, International Rescue Committee, Lutheran Immigration and Refugee Service, U.S. Committee for Refugees and Immigrants, United States Conference of Catholic Bishops/Migration and Refugee Services, and World Relief. These organizations are also known as Voluntary Agencies (volags) or Resettlement Agencies.

Each year, the President of the United States, after consulting with Congress and the appropriate agencies, determines the designated nationalities and processing priorities for refugee resettlement for the upcoming year. The President also sets annual ceilings on the total number of refugees who may enter the U.S. from each region of the world.

Since 1975, the U.S. has resettled over 3 million refugees, with annual admissions figures ranging from a high of 207,000 in 1980 to a low of 27,110 in 2002. The average number admitted annually since 1980 is 98,000.

Sex and Buddhism
What Buddhism Teaches About Sexual Morality
By Barbara O'Brien

Most religions have rigid, elaborate rules about sexual conduct. Buddhists have the Third Precept -- in Pali, *Kamesu micchacara veramani sikkhapadam samadiyami* -- which is most commonly translated "Do not indulge in sexual misconduct" or "Do not misuse sex." However, for laypeople, the early scriptures are hazy about what constitutes "sexual misconduct."

Monastic Rules

Monks and nuns, of course, follow the many rules of the Vinaya-pitaka section of the <u>Pali Canon</u>. For example, monks and nuns who engage in sexual intercourse are "defeated" and are expelled automatically from the order. If a monk makes sexually suggestive comments to a woman, the community of monks must meet and address the transgression. A monk should avoid even the appearance of impropriety by being alone with a woman. Nuns may not allow men to touch, rub or fondle them anywhere between the collar-bone and the knees.

Clerics of most schools of Buddhism in Asia continue to follow the Vinaya-pitaka, with the exception of Japan.

Shinran Shonin (1173-1262), founder of the Jodo Shinshu school of Japanese Pure Land, married, and he authorized Jodo Shinshu priests to marry. In the centuries that followed, the marriage of Japanese Buddhist monks may not have been the rule, but it was a not-infrequent exception.

In 1872, the Meiji government decreed that Buddhist monks and priests (but not nuns) should be free to marry if they chose to do so. Soon "temple families" became commonplace (they had existed before the decree, actually, but people pretended not to notice) and the administration of temples and monasteries often became family businesses, handed down from fathers to sons. In Japan today -- and in schools of Buddhism imported to the West from Japan -- the issue of monastic celibacy is decided differently from sect to sect and from monk to monk.

The Challenge for Lay Buddhists

Let's go back to lay Buddhists and the vague precaution about "sexual misconduct." People mostly take cues about what constitutes "misconduct" from their culture, and we see this in much of Asian Buddhism. However, Buddhism began to spread in western nations just as many of the old cultural rules were disappearing. So what's "sexual misconduct"?

I hope we can all agree, without further discussion, that non-consensual or exploitative sex is "misconduct." Beyond that, it seems to me that Buddhism challenges us to think about sexual ethics very differently from the way most of us have been taught to think about them.

Living the Precepts

First, the precepts are not commandments. They are undertaken as a personal commitment to Buddhist practice. Falling short is unskillful (akusala) but not sinful -- there is no God to sin against.

Further, the precepts are principles, not rules. It's up to us to decide how to apply the principles. This takes a greater degree of discipline and self-honesty than the legalistic, "just follow the rules and don't ask questions" approach to ethics. The Buddha said "be a lamp onto yourself." He taught how to use our own judgments about religious and moral teachings.

Followers of other religions often argue that without clear, external rules, people will behave selfishly and do whatever they want. This sells humanity short, I think. Buddhism shows us that we can release our selfishness, greed and grasping and cultivate loving kindness and compassion. Indeed, I would say that a person who remains in the grip of self-centered views and who has little compassion in his heart is not a moral person, no matter how many rules he follows. Such a person always finds a way to bend the rules to disregard and exploit others.

Specific Sexual Issues

Marriage. Most religions and moral codes of the West draw a clear, bright line around marriage. Sex inside the line, *good*. Sex outside the line, *bad*. Although monogamous marriage is the ideal, Buddhism generally takes the attitude that sex between two people who love each other is moral, whether they are married or not. On the other hand, sex within marriages can be abusive, and marriage doesn't make that abuse moral.

Homosexuality. You can find anti-homosexual teachings in some schools of Buddhism, but I believe most of these are taken from local cultural attitudes. My understanding is that the historical Buddha did not specifically address homosexuality. In the several schools of Buddhism today, only Tibetan Buddhism specifically discourages sex between men (although not women). This prohibition comes from the work of a 15th century scholar named Tsongkhapa, who probably based his ideas on earlier Tibetan texts.

Desire. The Second Noble Truth teaches that the cause of suffering is craving or thirst (*tanha*). This doesn't mean cravings should be repressed or denied. Instead, in Buddhist practice we acknowledge our passions and learn to see they are empty, so they no longer control us. This is true for hate, greed and other emotions. Sexual desire is no different.

In *The Mind of Clover: Essays in Zen Buddhist Ethics* (1984), Robert Aitken Roshi said (pp. 41-42), "For all its ecstatic nature, for all its power, sex is just another human drive. If we avoid it just because it is more difficult to integrate than anger or fear, then we are simply saying that when the chips are down we cannot follow our own practice. This is dishonest and unhealthy."

I should mention that in Vajrayana Buddhism, the energy of desire becomes a means for enlightenment; see "Introduction to Buddhist Tantra."

The Middle Way

Western culture at the moment seems to be at war with itself over sex, with rigid puritanism on one side and licentiousness on the other. Always, Buddhism teaches us to avoid extremes and find a middle way. As individuals we may make different decisions, but wisdom (prajna) and loving kindness (metta), not lists of rules, show us the path.

30476382R00051

Made in the USA
Charleston, SC
17 June 2014